THE THREE WORLDS

OF MAN

STRINGFELLOW BARR

The Paul Anthony Brick Lectures
Second Series
1963

University of Missouri Press • *Columbia*

Foreword

THE following series of lectures is the second under the Paul Anthony Brick Lectureship, established by the Board of Curators of the University of Missouri as a result of a generous grant by Mr. Brick to the University. The request of the donor was that the series be concerned with the broad field of ethics. The committee which administers the Lectureship has adopted the policy of allowing the individual speaker to determine his own selection and emphasis within this general area. Each series consists of three lectures given on the University of Missouri campus, and the supporting fund provides for the publication of the lectures. The first series, entitled *Morals for Mankind,* was given in March

1960 by Dr. Herbert W. Schneider. Published copies of these lectures are available at the University of Missouri Press. The Brick Committee hopes to continue the series into the indefinite future on an annual or a biennial basis, as good speakers become available, thus providing the general public with information concerning the manner in which some of the most eminent authorities are approaching the social and moral problems of our times.

A. CORNELIUS BENJAMIN
Chairman, Brick Committee

Preface

THE three chapters in this book reproduce with
some changes the three lectures I was privileged
to present at the University of Missouri in 1962 as
Brick Lecturer. In rewriting them, I have tried to make
good use of the help I received from my audience in
the discussion which followed each lecture.

I believe I am as interested as my distinguished pred-
ecessor in the Brick Lectureship, Dr. Herbert W.
Schneider, in the grave moral problems of the atomic
era. It was not the antiquarian interest of the historian
which drove me back in time for more than two mil-
lennia to the Greeks. It was because the Greeks, it
seems to me, still talk about many of our contemporary

problems more clearly than we do.

The Greeks who guided me most are Aristotle, in the *Nicomachean Ethics* and the *Politics;* Plato, in certain of his Dialogues, especially in the *Apology, Crito, Phaedo, Symposium,* and *Republic;* and the historians, Herodotus and Thucydides. If this small book of mine should drive any of its readers to read or re-read these works, I would feel its publication had been justified.

I recognize my debt to contemporary writers. In particular, I cannot imagine having written the third lecture but for the extraordinary insights in Simone Weil's *Intimations of Christianity among the Ancient Greeks,* which the Beacon Press published in 1958. Although her book and mine differ in purpose, hers illuminated passages in Plato for me that I had read often but with unseeing eyes.

Finally, I owe thanks for the warm hospitality the University of Missouri showed both me personally and the ideas I tried to present; for the invaluable aid I received in the preparation of this book from my research associate at Rutgers University, Mrs. Cary T. Peebles; and to Professor George Dennis O'Brien of Princeton University for reading my manuscript and giving me the benefit of his comment.

Princeton, New Jersey   STRINGFELLOW BARR
June, 1962

Contents

I
ACTION

IT has now become a truism that our generation is in moral crisis. One popular way of recognizing this fact has been to contrast our incredible progress in mastering nature with our apparent inability to master ourselves: we are, it is being said, scientific giants and moral pygmies. We are building bigger and bigger hydrogen bombs, but our statesmen tend to behave like juvenile delinquents. In 1960, when the editors of the Cambridge Modern History published a new volume, covering the period from 1898 to 1945, the title they chose for this history of my own generation's doings was "The Era of Violence." Those of us who were born in the nineteenth century have witnessed two world wars of unparalleled destructiveness, the horrors of the Russian Revolution, and the obscene sadism of Hitler's Fortress Europa. Our orgy of violence has all but destroyed the moral fabric of Western Christendom and has left us morally exhausted and confused. Meanwhile we prepare to conquer outer space and to construct through automation a horn of plenty, which could inundate us with material goods produced almost without the labor of man. Our political leaders assure us that neither side in the Cold War can win a thermonuclear struggle, and immediately step up the arms race in preparation for what is charmingly alluded to as "overkill." Mr. Lewis Mumford's comment on this program, even before America had built the world's first H-bomb, appeared in a letter published in *The New York Times:* "Gentlemen, you are mad."

Whether or not we are victims of mass paranoia, there is ample evidence that we are frightened and frustrated. And I suggest that our frustration springs in part from our growing conviction that, here in America at least, there has been some sort of moral deterioration; but that, worse, we do not know how to restore what we call our moral values. We know we have become not only the richest nation on earth but the richest in recorded history. We hear our insurance

companies warning us that overweight has become one
of our main health hazards, in a world community con-
spicuously underweight. We know that collusive profi-
teering and gross misrepresentation distinguish our
business life, that familiar ethical standards in our
learned professions have declined, that alcoholic escap-
ism disfigures our social life, that sloppy schooling and
broken homes handicap our children, that widespread
civic cowardice has supplied a field day for demagogues.
Meanwhile those who write our advertising copy praise
our self-indulgence, condone our cowardice, wink at
our cheating, and congratulate us on our folly. We are
not, of course, all agreed that we are the moral in-
feriors of our grandparents. Statistics on the morals of
any society are hard to come by; and, anyhow, in the
case of our recent forebears, we are suspicious of Vic-
torian hypocrisies.

Oppressed as we are by certain of our moral practices,
we are perhaps more oppressed by what feels like a
growing inability to distinguish between right and
wrong, on our own part and on the part of the society
we live in. It might profit us to remember that for
several decades we Americans, at least, have collected
enough shreds of anthropology and sociology to infer
that morals are only mores. We have also gathered, from
what Karl Marx is said to have said, that the belly, not

the mind or the will, dictates men's decisions; and this is a view that even our staunchest anti-Communists often appear to share with their chosen quarry. We have gathered, from what Sigmund Freud is said to have said, that the sexual desires of men are what dictate their decisions. These two beliefs, with perhaps a few tranquilizers added, can bring a kind of hard-won peace and even a night's sleep. Meanwhile, it is easy to see how our relativism in ethics has postponed any possible day of reckoning.

Nevertheless the apocalyptic turn that history has taken makes us wonder whether our day of reckoning may not after all have arrived; and, should we decide to start reckoning, it may be that we will reckon fastest with the help of the ancient Greeks. Morality and ethics, of course, have to do with the virtues and vices of man, and when it comes to these, we moderns are handicapped by a badly depreciated vocabulary. The words virtue and vice have become moralizing words. Virtue is something which women rather than men are admired for and sometimes lose. In short, the word carries no strong meaning except what was once discreetly called female chastity and may now suggest only a regretfully salvaged virginity. If it is a man who "saves his virtue," we are inclined to give a knowing wink and to make a sly allusion to Potiphar's wife. In Anglo-

Saxon countries, the word vice also carries sexual—as well as commercial—overtones.

But when a Greek talked about the four principal virtues, he enjoyed a double advantage over us. First, one of the meanings of the Greek word for virtue, *arete*, was skill; and the Greeks, like most men, admired skill. Secondly, educated men were agreed on which four skills the cardinal virtues were. They were courage, *andreia*, whose root meaning was manliness; temperance, which was self-control and bore on many matters besides alcohol; prudence, which suggested neither the Rock of Gibraltar nor life insurance nor a general stuffiness of mind, but did suggest sound judgment and practical common sense and mature behavior; and, finally, justice, a complicated virtue or skill, which included a Briton's notion of fair play as well as the notion of common honesty. These four skills were admired by the Greeks, and we admire them too when we are not repelled by the self-righteous mustiness their names have acquired in our everyday usage. Men who lack these virtues in whatever degree are to that extent cowardly, greedy, foolish, and crooked, four labels which nobody really wants to wear. And those who possess the vices of cowardice, greediness, lack of gumption, and crookedness, the Greeks would consider vicious whether they belong to a so-called vice ring in one of our large cities or merely live their petty, stumbling, ugly little lives in a pleasant suburb, admired and respected by neighbors who have not as yet caught on to them.

That the four cardinal virtues of courage, temperance, prudence, and justice should be necessary if we would play with skill the exciting game called life should astonish nobody. Those who lack courage cannot face up to the danger of pain, even if their reason tells them they ought to. Those who lack temperance cannot refrain from pleasure even if seizing on this pleasure is in their own better judgment unwise. Those men who lack both courage and temperance are guided through life as donkeys are, by the stick they fear and the carrot they long for, and they live a donkey's life, not the life of a man. On the other hand he who lacks prudence lives the life of a fool in his folly, a fool who appears to be unable to interpret what happens to him and therefore cannot learn from experience. And he who lacks justice constantly wrongs others, including even those whom he loves. All of them, by lacking one or more of these skills, are vicious men; for a vice is merely the absence of a virtue. The coward is vicious, the glutton is vicious, the fool is vicious, and the man who is normally unfair is vicious.

However, the Greeks found most men neither very

good nor very bad. Most men possessed one or more of these four skills in some degree. To the degree that they did, the Greeks found them virtuous. But to the extent that they could do no better, their skill was defective and they were vicious. Moreover, Aristotle stated even more explicitly and fully than most Greeks that these skills or virtues, like other human skills, such as running or swimming or playing some musical instrument, exist potentially in every man but require practice if they are to be counted on. They are, in fact, habits—habits of acting in a certain way. We moderns are usually more moved by the man who is habitually afraid in battle and nevertheless with great effort does one brave deed than by the man who, being habitually unafraid of the dangers which his reason tells him ought to be faced, performs the same deed with less effort. The Greeks no doubt rejoiced too when an habitual coward performed one brave deed. After all, that a coward should have taken the first step towards converting himself into a brave man is ample cause for rejoicing. In some sense, the sheep that was lost has been found. Besides, his rescue reassures the rest of us that every man is born with powers which can make him a good man. But the army sergeant who is making up a detail to carry out a dangerous mission may be excused for rejecting the coward who has acted bravely only once. The sergeant is looking for men who act bravely day in, day out, and can be depended on to act bravely. The Greeks, like the sergeant, called only those men courageous who habitually display courage. Those who usually play the coward they would classify as cowards and hence as vicious men. The coward has to perform brave acts frequently before these acts become habitual, before they become in a sense pleasant. Only when he has done that will he be a courageous man. The courageous man performs such acts promptly, knowingly, with minimal effort, and with the sense of satisfaction that any archer would feel in hitting a difficult target. Members of our generation often balk at this analysis, but it is possible that what they are really balking at is not the ideas involved but at those worn-out words, virtue and vice, with their now hazy connotations, and also at the worn-out names of the cardinal virtues.

It often helps to remember that we ourselves do not call a man a good tennis player merely because by heroic effort he clumsily manages to return a single difficult ball. Those we call good tennis players can return such balls with considerable regularity, gracefully and pleasurably. That, Aristotle is telling us, is how the truly courageous man performs courageous acts. All men are potentially courageous. That is, by nature they have the power to act courageously, as indeed they have the power to throw the discus afar. Only practice, and generally long practice at that, can actualize that power by giving them a habit to lean on. At such a point they are not merely potentially but actually courageous, by a sort of second nature. The virtuous man acts well, but he does so as the tennis player plays tennis, skilfully, gracefully, pleasurably. These are the ways in which the virtuous man faces those dangers that ought to be faced, or refrains from those pleasures he ought to pass by, or solves those practical problems that require solution, or takes his share of what needs to be divided, with no longing for more than his share.

In a very real sense the Greek, who loved skilful athletes, looked on the virtuous man as a well-trained moral athlete, able by second nature to cope with the moral problems life presents to all of us. The Greek ethical thinker looked on the virtuous man as essentially a man in good working order, and he looked on the vicious man as he looked on anything that functions badly, whether it be a lopsided wheel, a spear with a bent or broken point, or a leaking ship. The Greek ethical thinker could see nothing namby-pamby or negative in being in good working order, and he could see nothing admirable or positive in malfunction or lack of skill. Among other things, vice struck him as ugly, clumsy, loutish, and uncivilized. To be in good working order is to be happy.

Even if Aristotle was right that virtue is a habit of right action, a number of problems remain. One is a chicken-and-egg problem. If a coward wants to become a courageous man, how does he do it? Many men have asked themselves this question in agony of spirit. Aristotle's answer, we will tell our wistful coward, is to take the first step: to perform one brave action. But how can a man without courage "summon up his courage" even once? If courage can be acquired only by performing brave acts and if no man without courage can perform one, is the coward's case not hopeless? But Aristotle would remind us that a coward can indeed perform one brave act, long before he learns to act in that way habitually. Let him start with a small danger, as the jumper starts with a low hurdle. Let him slowly increase the height of the jump. Then he will form the habit.

There is, however, a second problem. If these habits, or virtues, which Aristotle discusses are reflex actions, then they have nothing to do with morality. Aristotle held that an act has moral content only if it is the product of a free, voluntary, rational choice. For this reason, we have no right to expect dogs to act morally, since they apparently cannot deliberate. It will suffice us if dogs behave enough like Pavlov's dog to enable us, when training dogs, to count chiefly on their reflex actions. We even train babies in this way; and if we understand what a moral act involves, we do not expect babies to be moral. Babies, like dogs, apparently cannot deliberate and choose the right action rather than the wrong one. If you would train them, you must do their deliberating for them and then enforce your decisions by appropriate rewards and punishments. The only difference is that, so far as deliberation goes, the dog has no future, and a normal baby has. For, strictly speaking, the baby has the power to deliberate, even though it is a power that age and experience have not yet actualized. It is a power, alas, that may never be actualized well, since we know that some persons remain morally babyish clear into adult life. If our baby requires a hypodermic injection, it is we, not he, who must decide that his arm shall be pricked. As he grows older, we must be on the alert to pass such responsibilities on to him, as soon as his own rational powers can take over the burden of accepting necessary pains for his body.

If virtue is a habit, but a habit of choosing freely and not a mere physical reflex—if, that is, only voluntary rational acts have any moral content, we must turn to the mind for the explanation of morality. And this raises a third problem: in the case of the four cardinal virtues we have already listed, is prudence somehow in a different category from courage and temperance and justice? Indeed, one is tempted to say that the man who possesses prudence, or good practical judgment, will also possess the other three cardinal virtues. Maybe courage is prudence with respect to danger and probable pain; temperance is prudence with respect to desire and probable pleasure; justice is prudence disinterestedly dividing what we and our neighbors must share. Yet, if prudence is somehow necessary for the man who would be brave or self-controlled or fair with others, observation seems to prove that a man can be prudent except where danger is concerned, at which point his cowardly fears seem to block off prudence from acting. Yet he will still show excellent judgment and ingenuity when he scents no danger. Apparently no fool can be truly brave or temperate or fair, even if his individual acts are by accident and on some occasions the same acts which a brave or temperate or fair man would perform; but a man may possess impressive practical judgment and still lack one of the moral virtues.

Prudence seems to come from firmly holding correct opinions about what is good for men and what is bad for them, from practical experience of life, from the information about many particular things which such experience brings, from an ability to deliberate well before acting. This deliberation involves what Aristotle called a practical syllogism.

In the syllogisms we most often remember from some course in logic, there is a major premise, such as the famous one that "All men are mortal"; a minor premise, such as the one that "Socrates is a man"; and the necessary conclusion: "Therefore Socrates is mortal." But in a practical syllogism the conclusion is not a third proposition; it is a moral action. Thus, if the major premise be true that "A man ought not to cheat his neighbor," and if the minor premise be true that "The business deal I propose would involve cheating my neighbor," then the practical conclusion of my practical syllogism is to drop the business deal in question, unless I would rather perform an unjust action and close the deal. If I shrug and say, "Business is business," I have of course revised my major premise to read: "A man ought not to cheat his neighbor except in a business deal." But even if I hold fast to my "principles," as we still say, my greed for profit has another outlet of a sort which greatly impressed Aristotle: I can challenge the minor premise by assuring myself that the principle does not apply to this particular case. The fellow is not, strictly speaking, a neighbor, and in any case if he is determined to do business he ought to keep his wits about him. Since he clearly doesn't, somebody else will skin him if I don't do it first. So why worry? Aristotle knew that there is nothing wrong with casuistry, the difficult and necessary art of applying general principles to particular cases. But he foresaw pitilessly that my greed would make me a highly prejudiced judge of my own moral actions. Having read numerous books on ethics, I could of course be counted on to endorse heartily the general proposition, the major premise. Why argue? I had better save my time and energy to rationalize my way out of the minor premise and thereby save the business deal in question—along with my high principles.

If we examine our own moral record, we are likely to recall those anguished moments just before we satisfactorily disposed of a minor premise and thereby avoided the pain we feared or secured the pleasure we longed for or handled the problem by our pet rule of thumb even though common sense had whispered that our pet rule would not work, or looked out for our own business interests without examining too closely how this injured an associate. We may also recall the intense, if restless, satisfaction that we had achieved our goal without consenting to classify ourselves either as poltroons or gluttons or fools or cheats.

Aristotle's analysis of the moral virtues as habits or skills which the good man has acquired presents perhaps a fourth problem. Since these habits depend on prudence, or good common sense, and since the prudence of what we call a practical man is based not only on holding firmly the correct opinions but on a certain experience of practical affairs, what happens if this experienced man confronts a situation so novel that his experience becomes irrelevant? We are not speaking now of reflex actions, which Aristotle properly rules out of ethics altogether. Nor are we speaking of a man whose experience has been too narrowly specialized to develop his power to act prudently in general. But supposing he is suddenly transferred to a society whose conditions of life are so different that courage or temperance or justice or prudence seems to dictate acts different from, or even opposite to, the acts they would dictate in his own society. Herodotus reported more than one case of this when he wrote his history of Persia's efforts to conquer Greece. By way of preparation he traveled extensively in Persia's polyglot empire, with its widely varying customs. And he was puzzled to find that what was considered a virtuous act in one country was often considered vicious in another.

But perhaps prudence can be overwhelmed without the prudent man's having to travel. Another historian,

Thucydides, records an era of violence in Greece itself that presented many an experienced, prudent Greek with such an unfamiliar world that his experience threatened to be irrelevant. Even the Spartans, whose reputation for moral virtues was the highest in all Hellas, could not make the transition, as the career of their great military leader, Lysander, eloquently testified. The good moral habits that seemed to operate in Sparta notoriously broke down when Spartans confronted novel conditions in foreign lands. And finally these habits broke down in Sparta itself. Courage was turning into brutality, temperance into covert self-indulgence, justice into mere force, and prudence into low cunning. How was a prudent man to act prudently in this unfamiliar, nightmare world? What was his kind of experience worth now? How was he to apply his principles to actual cases? As a matter of fact, they seemed so difficult to apply that more and more thinkers challenged the principles and suspected, as we now suspect, that all morals can be reduced to mores, that one man's "value judgment" is as good as another's, and that both the science of ethics and the science of politics must content themselves with being merely descriptive. But for Socrates, for Plato, and for Aristotle alike, both sciences were normative. The judgments both sciences made were objective, not subjective. The basic question each asked was not, What is being done? It was not, What would I prefer to do? The basic ethical question was, What ought I to do if I am to achieve happiness?

To answer that question, these thinkers turned their backs on relativism, subjectivism, and childishness. It is worth noting that the century in which Aristotle taught witnessed a change in the way Greek sculptors handled their renderings of children. They had been accustomed to portray boys as little men, but now they began to study boys as children. Can it be that they were glorifying childhood, as we do today? In any case, Aristotle did not glorify childhood, and many a modern reader has been shocked by his terse statement that no child can be happy. He means that no child has had time to develop the moral skills which men are capable of developing. That is, no child has had time to learn to use all his powers of moral choice in action. And it is the full use of men's powers that alone brings what Aristotle meant by happiness. He knew, of course, that the majority of men fail to develop these powers even when their bodies have matured. They remain morally childish and therefore unhappy.

Aristotle knew also that man cannot become fully man in isolation. By his nature he requires not only the family but the *polis,* the state, the City. For that reason man is a political, or polis-dwelling, animal. This means that although the thinker can write a treatise on ethics and another treatise on politics, as indeed Aristotle himself did, the two subjects are separable only analytically. In practice one is meaningless without the other. The state is a rational organization of moral agents, and the good state is one that releases and develops all men's powers, not only the physical powers which they share with other animals, but even more those powers which are possessed by man alone. Aristotle, therefore, wastes no time on picturing the human community as a collection of self-sufficient atoms, a collection which each atom has consented grudgingly to enter, out of enlightened self-interest. Many of our contemporary arguments about egotism versus altruism would therefore strike him as irrelevant. The personal happiness of each one of us is inextricably interwoven with the common good of all the members of our community. Human life is not a game of solitaire; it is more like a symphony orchestra. Since all of us long by nature to play in this orchestra, we do not in the bottom of our hearts want freedom from it, nor from the score which we jointly follow and which assigns us our respective parts, nor from the conductor.

Being a political animal by nature, man must live under law, not merely because law restrains but because good law teaches. As Simonides wrote, "Polis teaches man." Herodotus' history of the Persian Wars stirs us, but not because the freedom the Greeks died for was the freedom children dream of: the freedom to do whatever comes into one's head. Herodotus stirs us because those who fell at Marathon, at Thermopylae, at Salamis, died for the right to live under law rather than under whim and force. As Sparta's exiled king told Xerxes, the men from his small state would oppose Xerxes' vast army, alone if need be, because: "Free they are, yet not wholly free; for law is their master. . . ." (Herodotus VII, 104. Loeb.) Personal freedom can be found only in self-control, hence only by the man whose reason governs his passions; and a human community can find freedom for its members only when it lives under just laws of its own making. When both these conditions are met, man-in-polis can be free, precisely because his highest human powers are in use, precisely because he is functioning, and therefore happy.

Aristotle gives us in the *Nicomachean Ethics* a kind of manual on how we can develop in some measure the virtues of the good man; and in his *Politics* he gives us suggestions for increasing the amount of justice in existing states. On both points his is a counsel of moderation. Courage, he says, is a mean which lies between two extremes: cowardice and rashness. The state, he says, which finds itself torn between the interests of the rich and the interests of the poor can best avoid destructive revolution by increasing the power of its middle class. And Aristotle, who was a doctor's son, takes us through the hospital wards, so to speak, and shows us morally sick men and politically sick states. Because he was determined in the *Politics* to give practical and usable advice, he was often led to be over-dogmatic. For example, by and large, Greek women neither voted nor were educated. He declared them to be inferior to men, and on the average the women of Greece must have been such. But, to use one of his own key distinctions, were they inferior potentially, or were they only actually inferior? That is, were they inferior by nature or as the result of their more limited opportunities? On slavery he was ambivalent. Some men, he decided, were slaves by nature. Some, he admitted, though legally slaves, were nevertheless capable intellectually of being free men. But there are signs that his real defense of slavery lay in his belief that free citizens could not find the leisure to govern themselves unless they had slaves to wait on them. For the Greeks did not turn government over to elected representatives; they governed by town meeting, as it were, and governing took time. Aristotle tended to accept conditions as he found them and then to suggest better ways of meeting them.

Yet, if his reflections in the *Politics* sometimes seem scattered, what he says is often shrewd, often fecund. And always here, as in the *Ethics,* Aristotle is concerned with the life of action. For him as for other Greek thinkers the mind and the will, not the appetites, are the principles of human action. And when the minds and wills of the citizens jointly seek the common good of the polis, on which the good of each member of necessity depends, they will by an equal necessity establish institutions, make laws, and enforce them. These laws should always express reason and, wherever possible, should persuade the reason of the citizen. In order that laws shall be wisely drawn and in order that the citizen shall understand and freely obey them, Aristotle stipulates a system of public education. But since he knows that not all citizens will develop the moral virtues and discard the vices of moral childishness, he knows also that law must have the sanction of force and must win the consent of the childish by the rewards and punishments that govern children. He is especially concerned that the constitution of any given state shall be so adapted to the economic and social conditions of its citizens that it can save the state from the destructive violence of revolution. For repeated revolutions in the Greek city-states had proven that the moral virtues of most citizens crumble when law gives way to violence.

But if Aristotle saw how war and revolution corrupt morality, he never spoke of the fact with the eloquence of his master, Plato; and Plato never spoke of it with greater eloquence than when he ascribed his words to his own master, Socrates, whom he made the central speaker in his Dialogues. Why is this? Those men today who have lived through "the era of violence" are likely to suspect that one of the reasons is historical. When the Peloponnesian War broke out, Socrates was already thirty-eight; neither Plato nor Aristotle was born. When it ended twenty-seven years later with the fall of imperial Athens, Socrates had lived through the whole hideous tragedy of war, armistice, war again, repeated revolution, deportations, massacres, displaced persons, stateless persons, enslavements, mass rapes, treachery, fear, and hate. The very fabric of Greek civilization had been rent asunder, and it never wholly recovered from the brutalizing effects of violence. When the war ended, Plato was only twenty-five. He had never lived in a world which Socrates had known for almost forty years. Aristotle was still unborn. Aristotle lived in the kind of brutalized world that follows in the wake of violence, and this world asked far less of life than had the world which formed Socrates during the age of Pericles. It is true that the life of action, both moral and political, which Aristotle invites us to enter is a manlier, more human world than we are offered either by the sin-centered world of the Puritan or by the slack, sprawling, unbuttoned, self-indulgent world of the unthinking hedonist. It is a world governed largely by prudence—that is, by common sense and experience and good judgment. But Socrates had witnessed, as some of us today have witnessed, a more heartbreaking collapse than Aristotle ever beheld.

Remembering the lost vision, Socrates saw with searing clarity that the practical wisdom men call prudence had always been inadequate to its task. Practical common sense even in the great age of Pericles had shown unmistakable signs of not being genuinely practical. There were many opinions, including apparently correct opinions; but there sometimes seemed to be all too little knowledge. Perhaps some other kind of wisdom was needed if human beings were to lead truly human lives. Perhaps such moral virtues as courage, temperance, and justice were reducible in the end to knowledge; and perhaps without that knowledge no science of ethics could exist and workaday morality itself was doomed to wither, the violence of force and that other violence called fraud would replace it, and for men as for other animals only might would make right. Socrates' life became a search for that other kind of wisdom, perhaps the most famous search of its sort in recorded human history.

II

WISDOM

WE have discovered or have reminded ourselves that Aristotle did not think of a moral man in the way that most of us now do, merely as a man who refrains where the immoral man acts. On the contrary, he thought of the moral man as active and of the immoral man as passive. The moral man was active because his intellect, by following reason, directed his life. The immoral man was passive because his intellect allowed his passions to direct his behavior. That the passions are passive is not merely a matter of etymology. In these two words etymology is reflecting and reporting a logical connection. One does not have to be an ancient Greek in order to observe that the brave man, when faced with danger, continues to direct his own actions, while the actions of the coward are directed by the objects he fears. These force him. These frighten him into doing what he does. These make his decisions for him, as indeed they do for beasts. He himself does not so much act as react, in a blind effort to avoid pain. The fact that most men are partly moral and partly immoral beclouds the distinction for us. But insofar as we are brave we deliberately choose what to do when in danger, and it is we who act; insofar as we are cowards the men or things we fear do the choosing, and through the passion called fear we are acted upon.

For Aristotle, as for Socrates and Plato, the vicious man is so out of order that he cannot perform his *ergon,* his work, his function. This man who cannot do a man's work in the world was born with the powers all men are born with, but these powers were never actualized into habits of acting with skill. He has therefore never won citizenship in the moral world that is open to free men and that has never yet been open to dumb, driven cattle. Moreover, he is in a plight the cattle are not in: he has betrayed his nature where the cattle have not betrayed theirs, so that even when he sleeps his dreams will be less sweet than theirs. He has become morally deformed, which is something a contented cow, or even a discontented one, can never become. He is also more dangerous both to himself and to others than any cow can be, even the most violently discontented cow. For his intellect becomes the slave of his passions, and he can develop great cunning to serve evil ends.

What chiefly saved Aristotle from moralizing about this morally deformed, passive man was his insight that the moral virtues depend on prudence, or practical wisdom, for guidance. Indeed, from this point of view the morally vicious man is simply an impractical man. But where courage and temperance and justice are good habits of the will, prudence is a good habit of the intellect. Aristotle recognized that the will has powers which need to be actualized if we are to count on them. We must develop them into skills. We possess the powers by nature; we come to possess the corresponding skills by second nature. But apparently the intellect has a power too, which can be developed into a skill: prudence. And all of us can observe that the intellect has other powers, which some men have developed into skills, habits, virtues. Aristotle thought he observed the human intellect exercising five distinct skills, and he observed that two of these five intellectual virtues deal with the changing, material world; the other three deal with the immaterial and changeless world of ideas.

The two intellectual virtues that deal with the world

of the senses are art and prudence. By art Aristotle meant not only the fine arts, such as painting and sculpture, but the industrial arts as well. Indeed he meant skill in making, craftsmanship. This is a skill of the intellect, although its practice can of course inform and render obedient certain parts of the body, especially the hands. The object of any art is to bring into being something that did not exist before, to impose form on matter, to embody an idea in physical material. By the virtue of art the intellect makes.

Since prudence, the other intellectual virtue that deals with the material, changing world, guides the moral virtues, and since its relationship with them is so intimate, it is often thought of as itself a moral virtue. Its function is not to make but to do. Its fruit is the wise conduct of practical affairs, of deliberating, of choosing what is good for man, and of devising means to obtain that end. It is ingenious and resourceful. By early Greek philosophers it was often called simply wisdom. But one needs a special name like prudence, or practical wisdom, to distinguish it from that other kind of wisdom, philosophic wisdom. Prudence uses ideas and principles and theories, but it does not contemplate them, it applies them.

So much for art, the virtue which enables the intellect to make well, and for prudence, the virtue which

enables the intellect to deliberate well and to choose
well. But the other three intellectual virtues which
Aristotle saw at work in man focus neither on making
nor on doing, but on understanding, on discovering
the truth; and for that reason they do not deal with
changing matter but with unchanging ideas. One of
them, the virtue of science, is what we today commonly
call deduction. It is the developed power of building
a systematic body of knowledge by the process of deduction from first principles. Thus the science of geometry
can be entirely deduced from its first principles, the
axioms and postulates. Given these latter, the rest
follows necessarily. Indeed, the rest is implicit in these.

But where do we get the first principles from which
the virtue called science can deduce? By direct intuition,
Aristotle replied; by induction. For us this is a hard
saying, for the word intuition is almost as badly spoiled
today as the names of the moral virtues are. Intuition
tends now to be what women have and men infuriat-
ingly lack. Or it is what we call a hunch, an informed
guess. But not for Aristotle. The reason he holds that
the human intellect possesses a power called intuition
is that he believes he has witnessed its exercise, in himself and in others. This intuition is not discursive or
laborious like the virtue of science. It flashes. It leaps.
The Greek word for it also serves to denote the intelli-

gence of that Aristotelian God who rules the universe and who does not have to deduce, as the many gods of Homer and Hesiod and the other poets so humanly do. In men the intellectual virtue of science and the intellectual virtue of intuition both deal with the unchanging, eternal world of ideas.

But so does a third intellectual virtue, philosophic wisdom, a combination of intuition and science. Is philosophic wisdom the sum of these other two or their product? In any case it seems to be the joint action of both of them. It is not only the highest of intellectual virtues. Its exercise is man's highest act. To exercise the five intellectual virtues—art, prudence, science, intuition, and philosophic wisdom—and to exercise the moral virtues like bravery and temperance and justice and many less important moral virtues is to live well. Merely to possess them ready for use is to be a man in good working order.

But what is the working relation between the moral virtues and the intellectual virtues? Do the former depend on the latter, or is it the other way around, or is there some sort of mutual dependence?

We have seen that we must not expect to find a man capable of habitually moral conduct if he is deficient in prudence. That is why prudence, along with courage and temperance and justice, has traditionally been considered a cardinal virtue. But surely we will not insist also that to act well morally a man must possess philosophic wisdom. Or art. Are there not men who lack skill in making either beautiful or useful objects but who nevertheless exhibit excellent moral characters? Whether the lack of science, to the point of not being able to follow an argument, prevents a man from being moral may be a more difficult problem. Or turn the question the other way around. What of the stock character, a drunkard who nevertheless paints divinely? Does this case suggest that an immoral man can develop the intellectual virtues? We can discover by observation that many persons lack the courage to learn solid geometry or indeed to develop the intellectual virtue of science in any area. Learning can be painful, and cowards fear pain and avoid whatever produces it. Acquiring the intellectual virtues also interferes with earthier pleasures, and the intemperate lack the self-control to turn their backs on these pleasures in order to study. Apparently, moral vice can make it difficult to acquire the intellectual virtues in the first instance, whether or not it prevents us from retaining them, once we have acquired them.

Again, all of us believe we have witnessed great goodness in uneducated persons whose intellectual powers seem never to have been actualized into dependable intellectual virtues. Or were these persons really like well-trained but very young children, who in turn are like well-trained puppies and whose fear of punishment or hope of reward has formed in them reflex actions which give them the appearance of virtues they have not acquired—and, in the case of puppies, will never acquire? Or do these simple persons draw on grace from some source, grace which guides them in their deliberation and moral choice?

Aristotle, we have seen, insisted that the moral virtues are habits, which predispose those who possess them to perform the appropriate moral act. He also insisted that each of these habits can be formed only by repeating the appropriate moral act. Reading treatises on courage, he held, would not produce courage. Perhaps he would say that children and raw military recruits can be drilled into reflex actions which groove their characters as it were, so that these characters become less recalcitrant when reason commands them to act voluntarily with courage. It is a little as if animal training sufficed to get them in motion in low gear, because only then could real courage mesh and take them into high gear. Presumably both Plato in the *Laws* and Aristotle in the *Politics* gave law the ultimate sanction of force because some citizens might never learn to drive in high, or because, even if they did, their gears slipped. All these questions seem to revolve around the relation of the intellect and will to the body, a relation not without mystery. In any case, it was enough of a mystery to Aristotle to make him warn his readers not to expect ethics to be as precise a science as mathematics, and to remind them that the young could excel in mathematics but not in ethics. More than once he seems to warn us that ethical problems can be understood only from the inside, as it were: that courage, for example, can be really understood only by the courageous man. Aristotle presumably knew from experience that vice destroys the moral sense, so that vicious people quite commonly doubt the existence of virtue in others, even when it is exercised before their very eyes. The rascal tends to believe that every man has his price.

When, in Plato's Dialogues, Socrates faces the connection between the moral virtues and the intellectual virtues, he is far more drastic than Aristotle: no man, he announces, wittingly does evil. To this statement, Aristotle took strong exception. He was convinced that, by manipulating the practical syllogism to suit our desires—by rationalizing, as we would say today—we constantly do things which we know we ought not to do. But in dialogue after dialogue Socrates raises the question of whether virtue may not be reducible to knowledge. And the knowledge he seems to be talking about would have to involve not only what Aristotle called prudence, or practical wisdom, which applies correct opinion to the particular case; it would have also to involve philosophic wisdom, which goes beyond what is merely opined to what can be truly known. Behind moral failure lies intellectual failure, and in a sense all vice is a form of stupidity and ignorance. If our prudence had knowledge back of it instead of correct opinion, blindly held, we would not choose evil; we would not want to rationalize; we would obey our practical syllogism.

This faith of Socrates that true knowledge is the only soil in which moral virtue can be firmly rooted is consonant with the whole rhythm of his life. In his youth he shared the interest of the great Ionian philosophers in the nature of the physical universe around him and in the behavior of matter. But life turned his main interest towards ethics and politics, and he could not fail to observe that the moral corruption he saw underlying the magnificent age of Pericles was due less to men's failure to live up to their principles than to their increasing failure to descry the principles clearly. All men had opinions on virtue. And yet, when he questioned them in his gentle but relentless way, their opinions turned out to be merely opinions, not knowledge. They even turned out to be hopelessly inconsis-

tent opinions, as indeed opinions on moral problems
have a way of doing. But Socrates wanted to know, not
merely to opine. It seemed obvious to most men that
without knowledge of some sort there could be no
virtue, nor any moral act, but only anthropological
mores, enforced by the tribe. But true prudence deals
with specific means, chooses them with reference to
ends and often by the light of general rules. Granted
that it must frequently act even where it has only opinion to go on, yet it needs as much knowledge as possible.
But aside from the fact that good moral action needs
knowledge, knowledge is a good in itself. It is good
because man has the power, within limits, to know. As
Aristotle, the disciple of Socrates' disciple, would some
decades later declare in that first, daring, majestic sentence of his *Metaphysics*, All men desire by nature to
know. Socrates, who was by nature a man, certainly desired to know. This drew him towards ethics and politics, the sciences Aristotle would call practical sciences.
But it drew him also towards the theoretical sciences
like mathematics and beyond and above mathematics
towards metaphysics.

In Plato's *Republic* the Socrates who talks a night
away trying to grasp what justice essentially is seeks it
both in the soul of the individual just man and also in
a society of men living under just law. In both cases the

virtue men call justice turns out to be a proper ordering of functions. In a society there will be justice if the wisest citizens are Guardians, or rulers; if the next wisest, chosen for their courage, are the Auxiliaries, or professional armed forces; and if the rest of the citizenry content themselves with carrying on the economic process, in meeting the material needs of the entire community. If the peculiar virtue of the Guardians is their wisdom, and if that of the Auxiliaries is their courage, that of the business men and laborers is temperance. In some sense the three classes represent the mind, the strong right arm, and the bodily organs with their necessary appetites. Indeed, in the individual just man, his mind will govern, his obedient right arm will defend him with courage, and his physical desires will be controlled by their obedience to his mind. His wisdom, his courage, and his temperance are properly ordered to each other, and it is precisely this proper ordering which we have the right, Socrates thought, to call justice.

On the other hand, if the Auxiliaries, with their military love of honor, take over the function of rule from the Guardians, who alone truly know and love the good, injustice will pervade the society, an injustice of which the government's unjust acts will be merely outward and inevitable symptoms. If the third and lowest class gets power, the places of both wisdom and honor will be usurped by the new national goal of money, and eventually this glorification of the economic virtues will itself make way for the universal goal of pleasure, calling itself liberty and democracy. The reign of folly that ensues will throw up a tyrant. These types of government and the types of individual soul that correspond to them are described in the *Republic* undogmatically, imaginatively, with gaiety, with wit, and with high poetic insight. As the dialogue proceeds, Socrates weaves a magic skein of luminous analogies between the various types of unjust man and the various types of unjust state. But since, both in the individual soul and in organized society, a just ordering of the organic parts will all hang on the quality of wisdom that directs them, we are back again at the Socratic point that virtue depends in a special way on wisdom, a wisdom capable of transcending mere opinion and achieving knowledge. We cannot learn to be brave or temperate or just without this higher wisdom, for it is this wisdom that tells us which of our physical desires to follow and which we may not follow; it is this that brings to our souls the internal ordering in which Socrates saw justice. In short all genuine moral choices are guided by the high wisdom that knows principles, as well as by prudence about cases. That is why a brave act is wisdom acting with respect to danger; and a temperate act is wisdom acting again, this time with respect to pleasure; and a just act is wisdom acting with respect to the rights of other men about us. If this be true, then it is easy to see why Socrates in so many of the dialogues seems to suspect that all virtues are really species of theoretical wisdom as much as of prudence. Or, more baldly, that virtue is knowledge.

If virtue is indeed a matter of knowing and not merely of opining, then one man's opinion cannot necessarily be just as good as another's nor can the question of right and wrong be settled by moralizing from a chance assortment of value judgments. If there was one distinction Socrates felt competent to make, it was the distinction between knowing and opining. Indeed, his fame at Athens, as well as his death sentence, came from his constantly cross-questioning anybody who held an opinion and was willing to defend it by answering Socrates' searching questions. There would have been no point in this dialectic, as he called it, and no point in the anger it often aroused in those he questioned, if the dialectic had not had such shattering effects on so many men's most cherished opinions. Yet, surely nothing would have been shattered if all opinions were equally true.

Since the just state, like the just man, must be governed by wisdom, Socrates was especially concerned to find or produce wise Guardians for the state which he imagined, half earnestly, half humorously, as he and his young friends talked. He wanted his Republic to be ruled by its wisest citizens because he had seen what happened when fools governed. He wanted, therefore, to sketch in an educational system that would do two things: it would select out those who show a love of wisdom, and it would help this minority to grow in wisdom. The earliest stage of this system was basically the education that Socrates and his generation had gone through as boys: poetry and music to attune the soul, to awaken the imagination, and to teach the young how to listen; gymnastic to develop a strong and graceful body, able to serve the soul faithfully. Omit the poetry and music, and one would get the sluggish-minded, healthy athlete; omit the gymnastic, and one would get the effeminate aesthete. Socrates also advocated a kind of play in education at this early stage that reminds us of the modern kindergarten and even of what Americans call progressive education, although Socrates prescribed this playfulness only for the very young. He also proposed taking the young to points near the scene of battle during wars, to inure them to at least the sight of physical danger, a danger that brave men were properly facing.

After several years of this aesthetic and physical training the real business of education began. Those who showed promise moved on to several years of mathematics, to initiate them into the man's work of dealing with abstract ideas, not merely with aesthetic images that reflect and imply ideas. They were learning to live in two worlds at once, the world of things, where moral choices must be made and hence where the moral virtues must be acquired and exercised, and a world beyond things, beyond the senses, a world that can be entered only by the intellect. It is true that the ideas they dealt with were only the mathematical ideas, and there was an advantage to this restriction: ideas like that of a triangle or circle or sphere are easier to grasp clearly than moral or political ideas are. Thus, when Albert Einstein was asked why our generation had made so much more headway in physics than in politics, he answered promptly: Because physics is an easier science than politics. He was, of course, not talking about the art of getting elected to Congress but of how to invent and operate political institutions in an emergent world community that already threatened to commit suicide with nuclear weapons.

Those candidates for the class of Guardians who did well in these rigorous years of mathematical discipline became candidates for further and even more difficult explorations in the world of ideas, with a view to their joining the Guardians and fitting themselves to govern. The chosen few went on to several years' discipline in what Socrates called dialectic. This was the last stage of training to rule a state, and it can be described in at least two ways. On the one hand, it could be called the study of philosophy and sometimes more specifically of metaphysics. It explored the premises on which the mathematical sciences were built, premises which the mathematician took for granted when he deduced what necesarily followed from them. On the other hand, viewed as method, this dialectic was the kind of rigorous discussion that Socrates himself follows in the Dialogues, including the dialogue we are examining here, the *Republic*.

Let us postpone for a moment discussing this method and observe that when the Guardian finally reported for duty in the actual work of governing a state, he had learned among other things to practice the liberal arts, though in a sense now all but lost to memory. He had learned to handle the symbols men use when they think. These symbols fall into two main categories: words and such mathematicals as numbers and magnitudes. Symbols are of course things that refer to other things, whether the material objects our eye sees or those immaterial things that only our mind's eye can behold, things we call ideas. Socrates taught his candi-

date for a Guardianship four ways of seeing mathematicals and dealing with them, and named these four ways
arithmetic, geometry, music, and astronomy. He also
made it clear that he was not talking about the kind of
arithmetic we have taught in our schools in recent
decades or the kind of music we normally speak of
when we use the word music—or indeed the kind of
music he himself prescribed for his candidate when still
a child. The arithmetic the candidate studied was not
calculation but number theory. The music could perhaps best be likened to mathematical physics. The
astronomy was not descriptive but mathematical. The
great universities of medieval Europe would centuries
later still teach Socrates' four ways of understanding
mathematics; because these ways were four the universities called them the quadrivium. Socrates' candidate also had ample opportunity to practice the three
arts of handling verbal symbols: grammar, rhetoric, and
logic; and these became the three ways, or trivium, of
the medieval university. The trivium and the quadrivium literally added up to the Seven Liberal Arts.
And those seven liberal arts were counted on to liberate
man's mind by furnishing him with the intellectual
skills he would need if he sought truth in any field of
knowledge whatsoever. Far from being merely orna-
mental knowledge, they possessed, therefore, a high and

universal utility. Without them, law and medicine constantly tend to become trades, and the law school and the medical school tend to turn into trade schools, and the practice of law and medicine cease to be liberal professions and tend to become ways of making money, of doing business.

But what is the nature of the dialectic that Socrates prescribed as the final preparation of his Guardians if they would rule wisely and that he himself practiced while offering his prescription? It is fundamentally a kind of argument between two persons, but it is a kind rarely heard in Athens in his day and perhaps even more rarely in twentieth-century America. Most arguments then and now tend to be what Socrates called eristic. Now, the word eristic is derived from *eris*, the Greek word for strife. In eristic both sides are trying to win. In dialectic, both sides argue hard but not to win. They have a common goal: to find the true answer to the problem. For both sides may start off with a false or incomplete opinion. We may look to a sport like tennis to see the difference. Two men may play a tennis match in which each contestant is even more anxious to win than to play good tennis. Two other men may play, with each man trying to put up the best game possible, regardless of who wins. There is a quality of sportsmanship in this second way of playing. There is a quality of professionalism in the first way, whether money changes hands or not. In the first match only one player can achieve his purpose—a victorious score. In the second match both sides can achieve their common purpose— tennis playing of high quality. The first match has the quality of eristic but it has no common purpose. The second has the quality of Socratic dialectic and has a very high common purpose—good play.

The analogy between ways of arguing and ways of playing tennis is not yet exhausted. It takes at least two persons to play either game. Moreover, both kinds of tennis and both kinds of argument must be rigorously, not sloppily, scored. Again, if either side plays or argues eristically, defeat is likely to be bitter, since the defeated player gains nothing that he wants. Again, an eristic player is likely to assume that his opponent's goal, like his own, is the eristic goal, even if in actual fact his opponent is playing dialectically. Similarly, if the true dialectician seems to enough of his opponents to have won eristic victories from them he may find the silver cup he wins brimful of hemlock; he may, like Socrates, be ordered to drink it. When Socrates drank hemlock in his prison cell, no doubt many of those he had appeared to triumph over felt that at last they had triumphed over Socrates. Had he not met the greatest defeat of all—death? But Plato's *Crito* and *Phaedo* show

Socrates still playing his game of dialectic in his prison
cell with whatever friends came to call. His goal remained unchanged: the joint pursuit of truth through
the dialectical destruction of those false and inade-
quately examined and deeply cherished opinions which
men hold as truth itself. And when he won the cup
of hemlock, he willingly drained it, hoping to gain
entrance to some place where he could play his game
of dialectic with great players who had lived in Hellas
long before and had preceded him to that other place.

If we read Plato's Dialogues and listen to Socrates
himself practice dialectic, we observe that his preferred
method is to ask short questions and to encourage short
answers. This cross-examination tests his opponent's
opinion somewhat as a laboratory scientist tests his own
or another's hypothesis. But over and over again in the
Dialogues the person questioned grows violent, raises
his voice, and substitutes for the short answer the long,
vague, rhetorical speech. As signs multiply that his
opinion is about to be refuted, and out of his own
mouth at that, he fears personal disgrace. This con-
fusion between refutation and disgrace is perhaps reflected by the Greek word *elenchos*, which, depending
on its gender, means either refutation or disgrace. The
basic trouble, of course, is that Socrates' sparring partner views the encounter in terms of eristic and fears

defeat. But for Socrates the testing of the opinion is the goal, and it is not important who happens to be the opinion's advocate. If the opinion fails, it will be logic, not Socrates, which condemns it.

The psychic panic of his sparring partner Socrates meets with a well-nigh unique combination of courtesy and irony. The irony offers his interlocutor two choices: to continue eristically or to learn to discuss dialectically. His almost caressing courtesy invites precisely this shift. It is worth observing how many modern readers mistake the irony for sarcasm and the courtesy as adding insult to injury, because many modern readers have never made the shift themselves from eristic to dialectic. The courtesy of Socrates is a kind of conversational non-violence, a soft answer to turn away wrath, a non-violence that accepts insult with humility and permits true intellectual encounter. Jesus of Nazareth's injunction to turn the other cheek likewise provides the necessary condition for true encounter. Mahatma Gandhi once advised that in any altercation we should ascribe to our opponent the noblest motives capable of explaining his action. Jesus was surely aware that turning the other cheek could not automatically destroy the hate or anger of an assailant: it merely provided the condition the assailant needed if he was to change from assailant to friend. Gandhi surely knew that his opponent's motives might be low and not at all noble. But to assume they are low, as most men habitually do, is to drag down the level of discussion when it sorely needs dragging up. This non-violence of Jesus and of Gandhi in Socrates takes the form of always assuming that what his dialectical opponent says makes sense and then of trying by question to elicit that sense. This is a very high and lamentably rare form of courtesy. Many of us have congratulated ourselves for not telling our opponent to his face that he was a fool, or at least that his remark was foolish. But did our voice or our choice of words when we replied wholly conceal our real opinion?

Socrates, however, had three perfectly valid reasons for formally assuming that what his opponent said was true but that he himself had not fully grasped its meaning. First, Socrates may not have caught the words correctly. Second, he may have caught the words but at the same time have misread their intended meaning. Third, by adopting this second hypothesis and subjecting his opponent's statement to the dialectic question, both he and his opponent may shortly discover whether the statement is true or false, or in what measure and in what sense it is true. His formal initial assumption provided the necessary condition for full dialectical encounter and for a jointly fruitful search.

Perhaps every man who converses needs to make the same assumption Socrates made, though few men do.

The long dialectical training of the Guardians doubtless gave opportunity to discuss practical questions, but it is clear from Socrates' account in the *Republic* that many of the questions would be purely theoretical. If Socrates was right in suspecting that virtuous action follows true knowledge, somewhat as modern technology depends on pure science, then those who intend to govern a state capable of nurturing virtue in its citizens cannot afford the luxury of focusing always on the practical. For without good theory neither governor nor governed can know what is genuinely practical, can know which political action is wise and which action is merely clever. The Socratic Guardian did not participate in government until he had dealt with high theory and had even learned the art of contemplation; and when his tour of duty in practical administration had ended, it was to high theory and to contemplation that he returned. Socrates showed when he spoke to his young companions of this theory and this contemplation that he did not expect them to understand wholly what he was talking about. Nor did they, any more than the Ionian soldiers at Potidaea could guess what Socrates was thinking about when he stood for a whole day and a night, pondering; any more than a healthy child can guess what a grown man is doing when he sits lost in thought. But presumably Plato knew, when he founded the Academy. And Plato's disciple, Aristotle, knew; for, despite his strictures on Plato's *Republic*, Aristotle boldly declared that "the activity of contemplation" is the highest and most godlike activity man is capable of. This much is certain: neither Socrates nor Plato nor Aristotle would suppose that the only point of thinking is to guide practical action. The act of thinking in their view is the highest and most important of human acts. Contemplation, the least practical form of thinking, is also its highest form. Deliberation, which is thinking with a view to action, although a lower form, is nevertheless a necessary one. For without deliberation and rational choice no moral action can take place, and so long as man's soul inhabits a body, a material body moving among other material bodies, moral action there must be, and political action too.

To learn, then, to deal with ideas is the necessary preparation for governing a state, since a state is composed of citizens, and since citizens are men, and since men are moral agents. This reasoning lies behind what is possibly Socrates' most famous parable, in the *Republic* or in any other dialogue—the parable of the den, or cave. So long as any man mistakes the material universe around him for essential reality, he is like those prisoners in the cave whose necks are chained in such a way that all they ever see of the objects carried past and behind them is the shadows cast on the wall in front by the uncertain light from a fire. Only if the prisoners' necks are unchained can they turn around and see the real objects, the true causes of the shadows. And only the sort of liberal education that will turn us around intellectually, that will therefore con-vert us from vague opinion about the things our senses perceive to the abstract ideas which material objects embody and which only our intellects can see—only this conversion, by means of the liberal arts, will enable us to rise above our confused opinions into clear knowledge. Moreover, just as those prisoners must next be led up and out of their cave where they can see objects in bright sunlight and at last learn to look even on the sun itself, so must the Guardians of Socrates' ideal republic, through their long discipline in dialectic, leave the cave we all live in, and behold ideas even more clearly. Last of all—and with a daring on Socrates' part that makes us either giddy or incredulous, depending on how sure we are that we already know whatever contemplation has to teach—just as the prisoner learns to look directly at the sun, so the Guardian must look at the idea of the Good. It is not hard to see why Socrates chose to convey this analysis of liberal education by poetic metaphor. There was little in the personal experience of his audience that had prepared them to understand a more analytical exposition. He was in the embarrassing position of a man trying to describe a symphony to one whose musical experience has been limited to jazz. It was not the only time Socrates turned to metaphor, and hoped.

When all of these difficulties have been recognized, it still seems important that our generation turn to Plato's and Aristotle's ethical works in order to learn or recall that it is idle to talk about morals or the decline of morals without taking full account of the powers of the human intellect. When American colleges and universities are warned not to be too intellectual but to train the whole man, they might well pause before they try to give young men and women of eighteen to twenty-two the training their parents should have given them when they were four or five. As their offspring began to show signs of reason, these parents might then have helped them shift into higher gear. Colleges and universities were not established in the first instance to teach the moral virtues, but to teach the intellectual virtues. If their students' moral health, or for that matter psychological or physical health, is so poor that they cannot reasonably be expected to acquire the intellectual virtues, they had best be invited to resign and either go home or go to a hospital.

One suspects that the desire of some parents and even of some professors to have the university train character —that is, teach the moral virtues—reflects a widespread lack of faith in our country in the human intellect and in its power to apprehend truth. In the absence of such faith, the parent will hardly ask an institution of whatever sort to develop the intellectual virtues of his son or daughter. There is nothing left to develop except his moral character and his body. In addition he can be supplied with useful information, and small talk about the liberal arts, in the contemporary sense of the phrase—useless but decorative knowledge. He can go in for college activities to supplement what we may call the passivities of the lecture hall. He can make social contacts, which may later be business contacts. He—or she—can even find somebody to marry. But the essentially Greek dream of a university will be missing: a place designed to get intellects in motion, a place therefore in which intellects learn to act.

In such a place the student might have experienced in at least some small degree what Aristotle selected from his own experience as man's highest happiness: intellectual activity, not directed towards the means for achieving one's ends but towards the discovery of ends which it is worth finding the means of achieving.

As for social contacts, he might have learned with Aristotle to distinguish between three forms of friendship: useful contacts, amusing companionship, and a common striving for the good. In a college devoted to the development of the intellectual virtues he might have found friends of this third type.

If he ever found such friends, he might recapture the vision of the common good which the Guardians of the Republic sought, the vision of the common good that moved the founding fathers of our own American republic. He might go further: he might see, as Herbert Schneider saw in the Brick Lectures he delivered in 1960, that the emergence of a world community for the first time in human history poses a new problem for every fully mature, and hence morally responsible, man or woman: a reformulation of the common good. Since man is by nature a political, or social, animal, he needs his neighbors for at least two reasons. Economically, he needs a division of labor to achieve even his animal well-being, and the European Common Market is one of the products of that need today. But he also needs to exchange ideas with his neighbor, to engage in Socratic dialectic with him. In short, he needs him not only as a useful social contact, not only as a pleasant companion, but as a fellow-seeker for the truth and for the common good of whatever community they both belong to. Our so-called cultural exchanges with foreign lands, lands that grow less foreign every day, reflect by a still uncertain light our need of our friends abroad both as pleasant companions and as fellow-dialecticians. For we and they, though animals, are also more than animals. They and we need bread, but neither they nor we can live by bread alone. To live our lives in their full economic, moral, and intellectual dimensions, we need the men and women whom modern technology has made our neighbors. The Peace Corps our government has sent out in the great American tradition of lending a hand to one's neighbors has indeed the function of teaching. But history may guide it into teaching more Socratically than most of us intended when it was organized. Socratic dialectic suggests that no man can teach another unless he stands instantly ready to learn from him. No man can teach in the high sense of that great word without full and loving encounter with whomsoever he tries to teach.

Let us suppose for a moment that the Greeks have convinced us that we cannot live a fully human life without acquiring both the moral virtues and the intellectual virtues. Let us even suppose that we acquire both sets of virtues; will the Greeks then reveal still other virtues we will need if we are to achieve genuine happiness? Centuries after Aristotle, the Christian

Church proclaimed that we need three more virtues, virtues of which St. Paul wrote in his First Epistle to the Corinthians, virtues which Christian theologians would call the theological virtues, virtues which we can acquire only by God's grace. Had the pre-Christian Greek philosophers any intimation that man needs these virtues too if he is to live a fully human life?

III

GRACE

A century ago many Christians, unsure of their own religious faith, turned to Socrates as to a sort of secularized Christ. Like Jesus of Nazareth, Socrates was a revered teacher, a man who turned his back on worldly goods, who loved the truth that sets men free, a man who was falsely accused, who rejected chances to ignore the truth in order to save his life, and who was unjustly condemned and executed. But, in addition, to the secularized Christian the Athenian offered many advantages over the Nazarene: he performed no miracles, his disciples laid no claim to a resurrection after death, nor did they later consider him an incarnate god. And although the Socrates of Plato's Dialogues often spoke in parable, he was also a skilled debater who seemed to attach less importance to belief than to rigorous demonstration. He was not a prophet; he was a philosopher. Indeed, the nineteenth-century rationalist discerned in him a fellow rationalist with only a decent and vague respect for the gods of his fathers.

The relevant texts, however, simply do not support the picture of a rationalist Socrates, free of deep religious beliefs. Socrates certainly rejected much of the religious folklore in Homer and Hesiod. The many gods of his fathers often seem, in his thinking, to become one god. To what extent this religion was Plato's rather than his, we cannot know, any more than we can know to what extent the Socrates of the Dialogues expressed his own philosophy on other matters or served rather as mouthpiece for the philosophy of Plato. The Socrates of the Dialogues was religious but he was also an extraordinarily subtle philosopher and he was never simple-minded or flat-footed about his religious insights. He operated in a religious tradition that, at its best, had always opened the mind of man, not closed it. It was a tradition of divine intervention in human affairs, of gods who listened to human prayers, and of men who strove, sometimes in wise ways and sometimes in foolish ways, to resemble gods. It was a tradition which persistently pictured religious experience as ambiguous: he that hath ears to hear, let him hear. The gods frequently appeared to men. But in an extraordinary proportion of such theophanies, the god was clothed in mist or was disguised either as some friend of the man to whom he appeared or as a bird or beast. It was as if the god always allowed the unbeliever his unbelief; invited, but never insisted on, recognition.

When Homer in the *Odyssey* reported how the goddess Athena guided Odysseus' son Telemachus to Nestor's palace to seek news of Odysseus, Homer wrote that Athena appeared to Telemachus disguised as his tutor, Mentor. When the young Telemachus feared to meet the most eloquent of all the Achaeans who had fought at Troy and when he complained that he himself was "as yet all unversed in subtle speech," (Homer: *Odyssey* III, 23. Loeb.) the goddess of wisdom answered him: "Telemachus, somewhat thou wilt of thyself devise in thy breast, and somewhat heaven too will prompt thee." (Homer: *Odyssey* III, 26-28. Loeb.) It was perhaps because the thinker Socrates always accepted full responsibility for devising somewhat in his own breast that the nineteenth-century rationalist saw him as freed from religion. But perhaps it was precisely because Socrates trusted the gods to prompt him that his mind dared soar so high.

When Hesiod sang of the gods, he was prompted by the Muses, daughters of Zeus, who also went about "veiled in thick mist," (Hesiod: *Theogony*, 9, Loeb.) and danced on soft feet and taught Hesiod what to sing, as he was shepherding his lambs on holy Helicon. Indeed, the old epic poets like Homer and Hesiod counted on the Muses to inspire in them, or breathe into them, the divine wisdom that no poet could devise in his breast unaided.

As with poets, so with all men. If they are to live, not as dumb brutes but as mature men, if their lives are to signify, to be signs of something higher than their purely human powers can reach, divine grace must be shed on them. "Creatures of a day," wrote Pindar, "what is anyone? What is he not? Man is but a dream of a shadow; but when the Zeus-given gleam of sunlight comes, a radiance rests on men, and a gentle life." (Pindar: *Pythian Odes* VIII, 95-7. Author's translation.) Was this the radiance that rested on Socrates, the radiance that Alcibiades so eloquently reported, the radiance that infused in Socrates the extraordinary gentleness which the reader of the Dialogues detects behind those painful, incisive questions of his?

It was in the tradition of Homer, Hesiod, and Pindar that Socrates searched for the answer to the question,

What is man? It is possible, of course, to say that
Homer, Hesiod, and Pindar are poets, not philosophers.
But Socrates himself, far from rejecting poetry as irrelevant to the philosophic enterprise, constantly turned to
it for those insights which guide the enterprise. He constantly showed his awareness that there were more
things in heaven and earth than were dreamt of in the
philosophy of some of his contemporaries. He would
doubtless have agreed with his disciple, Plato, that "in
truth every man ought always to begin his speaking and
his thinking with the gods." (Plato: *Epistle* VIII, 352E-
353A. Loeb.) Certainly, he began and ended his speaking and his thinking with them, as in the lovely prayer
that closes Plato's *Phaedrus,* or when he had made his
defense in court against the charge of atheism and
ended with the words: "And to you and to God I commit my cause, to be determined by you as is best for
you and me." (Plato: *Apology,* 35D. Jowett.) And again,
when he had received the sentence of death, and reminded those who voted for that sentence that it was
really they whom it condemned; when he had tried to
explain to those who had voted for acquittal what the
trial meant; and when he spoke his farewell: "The hour
of departure has arrived, and we go our ways—I to die,
and you to live. Which is better God only knows."
(Plato: *Apology,* 42. Jowett.)

A candid reading of his defense, which Plato heard and recorded in his dialogue, the *Apology*, can leave no doubt that the frequent references to "the gods" or to "god" are no mere manner of speaking and even less a shrewd attempt to parry the charge of atheism. Quite literally, Socrates spoke in deadly earnest. And he spoke in that way when he declared: "For I do believe that there are gods, and in a sense higher than that in which any of my accusers believe in them." (Plato: *Apology*, 35D. Jowett.) That his words habitually left open the choice between monotheism and polytheism is less important than that he had dedicated his life from his youth up to following the divine will as he understood it. His life had been lived in the faith that the moral virtues can have little meaning without the intellectual virtues, but it was lived also in the faith that even these highest natural powers of man need to be crowned by other powers which can come only by grace, by the free gift of God. To live well, a man must act well, think well, and pray well. He had faith that one of the modes of prayer, if not indeed its chief mode, was to make oneself an attentive instrument for God's will.

We have noted that Socrates listened intently to men as well, even to men who appeared to be foolish and arrogant. His dialectical questioning, which proved too painful for even an Athens to bear, depended on his purging himself of intellectual arrogance and on his really listening. There was indeed irony in his questions. But it was never sarcasm. It was the irony of the teacher, who leaves his listener free and therefore, necessarily, offers him a genuine choice between further folly or a recognition of error. And along with the irony went the most loving courtesy. Perhaps it was only love that enabled him to listen even to fools, that enabled him, if not to learn from fools, at least to learn with them. Or perhaps it was less that love enabled him to listen than that listening intently enabled him to love. Certainly, it helped him to love cleanly and without sentimentality or mutual flattery.

Surely there is a connection between this listening love which he offered those he talked with and the listening love he offered God. In both cases there is his eternal question: What precisely does he mean? To love God and one's neighbors in this fashion; to have faith that both God and one's neighbors are really there to be encountered, to be wrestled with, to be at least in some measure understood; and to have hope, expressed at his trial and in his prison cell, that when this mortal coil is shuffled off, one will in some other life encounter, wrestle, and understand far better—this faith, this hope, this love perhaps depended on the grace which he believed that God accorded men. No early poet of Greece knew better than Socrates that the gods, when they come to men, are commonly clothed in mist or wear a disguise; that though heaven prompts men, this will not exempt men from their responsibility to devise somewhat in their own breasts, from using the purely human powers the gods have given them. But try as man will, it seemed clear to Socrates that man, when compared with God, is what Pindar indeed saw him to be: a mere creature of a day, a mere dream of a shadow, until the Zeus-given gleam of sunlight comes and a radiance rests on him, and a gentle life.

Although Plato's Dialogues are replete with passages that exhibit Socrates emptying himself of hybris and self-will and clamorous appetite in order that he may truly and lovingly listen both to God and man, these passages have to be lovingly listened to by the reader, and wrestled with. If we have not acquired the knack of Socratic listening when we read Plato and have acquired instead the knack of not seeing such passages or of explaining them away, we might get help from whence the Greeks themselves got help: from Delphi. Delphi has a high relevance to the problem of grace and to God's gift of an understanding heart, and it also has a high relevance to Socrates personally. Of all the shrines where God, or the gods, spoke to the Greeks,

Delphi was easily the most famous. At Delphi Apollo made known to men the will of his father Zeus. But even before Socrates was born, the priests of Apollo had been charged with accepting bribes from petitioners, and it seems likely that such corruption did occur. One cannot, of course, infer from this fact that the whole procedure was fraudulent, any more than the corruption which often disfigured the papacy will tell us whether Jesus Christ is in fact the Son of God. Again, a favorite subject for questions to Apollo was where to establish a new colony. Even if one assumes that Apollo never existed, Delphi was a clearing-house of information of all sorts, and its priests most likely knew without divine inspiration a good deal more about opportunities for would be colonists than most of these would-be colonists knew. But neither will this last fact tell us whether any of the advice that issued from Delphi came from Apollo himself. Finally, Delphic oracles might be simple and direct or couched in ambiguous, poetic language. (See H. W. Parke and D. E. W. Wormell, *The Delphic Oracle* [2 vols:, Oxford, Blackwell, 1956].) It has often, therefore, been proposed that the "oracular" style of these latter communications was so designed that a prophecy could later be justified no matter how events might fall out. But here, again, Homer is also often oracular, and so is Socrates. In fact, the poetic, intuitive utterance tends to strike the literal-minded as oracular, ambiguous, evasive. There are more ways than one of explaining the oracular style of so many Delphic oracles. Socrates himself suggested that an oracle is a sign, and signs have to be read, have to be interpreted. Is it possible that some Delphic oracles derived their ambiguity from a kind of Socratic irony, designed to make men examine their opinions and desires more closely? After all, the command ascribed to Solon of Athens, "Know thyself," was inscribed at Delphi for all petitioners to see. These are words that invite men to purge themselves of arrogance and self-will, to listen, and perhaps to question further.

Herodotus supplies us with an instructive case of an oracle impulsively misread. Croesus, King of Lydia, sent emissaries with enormous offerings of gold and silver to Delphi to ask Apollo whether he should attack the Persian Empire of Cyrus the Great. Apollo replied that, if he did, a great empire would fall. Croesus eagerly inferred that it was the empire of Cyrus that would fall; he attacked—and lost his own empire. He was put in chains. But Croesus persuaded Cyrus to let him send his chains to Delphi and to ask Apollo whether it was the god's custom to deceive those who served him well. Apollo's priestess thereupon pointed out to Croesus' emissaries that Apollo had said only that "a great em-

pire" would fall; Croesus should have asked him whether that empire was his own or Cyrus'.

When Socrates' young friend, Xenophon, was asked
to join the ill-fated Ten Thousand whose adventures
Xenophon related in the *Anabasis*, he asked Socrates
before he ever left Athens whether he should join the
Ten Thousand. Socrates advised him to go to Delphi
and ask Apollo. Xenophon went to Delphi, but put a
different question to Apollo. Instead of asking whether
he should go, he asked what god he should sacrifice to
in order to make his venture both safe and successful.
Socrates rebuked him for changing the question; instead
of trying to learn the will of Zeus, Xenophon had in
effect asked how he could conscript Zeus or some other
god to serve his own will.

Socrates' way of following truth and of following
God was most characteristically shown by what may
have been his first encounter with the Delphic Apollo.
When Socrates was still young, a disciple of his named
Chaerephon traveled to Delphi and asked Apollo
whether any man was wiser than Socrates. Apollo
replied that no man was wiser. Speaking some decades
later, at his trial, Socrates related this human question
and this divine answer and also his own reaction to
them: "When I heard the answer, I said to myself,
What can the god mean? and what is the interpretation

of his riddle? for I know that I have no wisdom, small or great. What then can he mean when he says that I am the wisest of men? And yet he is a god, and cannot lie; that would be against his nature. After long consideration, I thought of a method of trying the question. I reflected that if I could only find a man wiser than myself, then I might go to the god with a refutation in my hand. I should say to him, 'Here is a man who is wiser than I am; but you said that I was the wisest.'" (Plato: *Apology,* 21B-C. Jowett.) He went to many men—prominent politicians, famous philosophers, poets, common artisans—but he never had occasion to go to the god because he never had a refutation in his hand: the men he went to did indeed know many things but they clearly thought they knew many other things they did not know. In that sense, Socrates decided, they were even less wise than himself, who at least knew that he did not know. The men he went to were angered that his questions led them to contradict themselves; and this accumulated anger, in Socrates' opinion, prejudged him when he came to trial years later. As to the opinion of some men that he himself really was wise, he shrewdly guessed that this was because "my hearers always imagine that I myself possess the wisdom which I find wanting in others: but the truth is, O men of Athens, that God only is wise; and by his answer he intends to show that the wisdom of men is worth little or nothing . . . And so I go about the world, obedient to the god. . . ." (Plato: *Apology*, 23A-B. Jowett.)

When Crito visited Socrates in his prison cell and tried to persuade him to permit his friends to bribe his jailors and get him safely out of the country, Socrates first played his habitual game of dialectic with Crito until Crito admitted that Socrates was right to decline to escape, and then Socrates ended the dialogue with the gentle command: "Leave me, then, Crito, to fulfil the will of God, and to follow whither he leads." (Plato: *Crito*, 54E. Jowett.) For he himself had just obeyed one of his own favorite exhortations when practicing dialectic with anybody: to follow whithersoever the argument leads. He trusted dialectic to lead him towards truth and not away from it, even if the truth destroyed his own preconceptions. He trusted the will of God to lead him where he ought to go, even if God in the process should choose to destroy his follower's body. He rejected the eristic that would ignore the unknown truth that might lie ahead in order to win assent to a view already held. He rejected the worldly-wise actions that would ignore God's will, even if such actions might mean saving his own life. When he accepted the purgative effects of dialectic, he did so with no advance assurance that he would attain to some greater happiness through truth, but he hoped he would attain to such happiness and he had faith that he would, for he loved truth. When he accepted the sentence of death that seemed to follow from his duty to obey God, he had no assurance of immortality, but he hoped for immortality and had a kind of faith in immortality, for he loved God and chose freely to follow whither he might lead.

If Socrates' whole life was a mission laid on him by God to follow the argument whithersoever it might lead, even if to his own death, the daily decisions he faced were also subject to divine guidance. He had, he testified in court, "an oracle or sign which comes to me, and is the divinity which Meletus ridicules in the indictment. This sign, which is a kind of voice, first began to come to me when I was a child; it always forbids but never commands me to do anything which I am going to do." (Plato: *Apology*, 31D. Jowett.) And, when he had been condemned to death, and was bidding farewell to his judges, he observed: "Hitherto the divine faculty of which the internal oracle is the source has constantly been in the habit of opposing me even about trifles, if I was going to make a slip or error in any matter; and now as you see there has come upon me that which may be thought, and is generally believed to be, the last and worst evil. But the oracle made no sign

of opposition, either when I was leaving my house in
the morning, or when I was on my way to the court, or
while I was speaking, at anything which I was going to
say; and yet I have often been stopped in the middle
of a speech, but now in nothing I either said or did
touching the matter in hand has the oracle opposed me.
What do I take to be the explanation of this silence?
I will tell you. It is an intimation that what has happened to me is a good, and that those of us who think
that death is an evil are in error. For the customary
sign would surely have opposed me had I been going
to evil and not to good." (Plato: *Apology* 40A-C. Jowett.) The "internal oracle" in this passage translates
Socrates' word, *daimon*, a divine spirit which played the
role of guardian angel to Socrates. The "customary
sign" is Jowett's rendering of "the god's sign." And in
Plato's *Republic* Socrates calls it the divine, or heaven-
sent sign, and says "I suppose it has happened to few or
none before me." (Plato: *Republic* VI, 496C. Loeb.)

It may be worth observing the parallel between the
guidance the *daimon* gave him in his attempt to be
"obedient to the god" and the guidance dialectic gave
him. The *daimon* never told him what to do; it only
vetoed certain acts; and in any number of his exciting
dialectical encounters, his cross-questioning did not tell
him what opinion was true; it only, through a reduc-

tion to absurdity, made it logically impossible to hold the opinion which his dialectical opponent had been vainly defending.

Secondly, it is worth observing also that the oracle which Chaerephon brought back from Delphi, to the effect that no man was wiser than Socrates, presents another parallel with dialectic. The dialectical process that so angered self-important Athenians did indeed often end only in another question, but it was likely to end with a better question than the one with which the discussion had started. Chaerephon's oracle started a chain of questions too, questions which Socrates kept asking until the day he drank the hemlock. Most men, like Croesus of Lydia and like the young adventurer, Xenophon, believe they know the right questions and want only an answer, preferably an answer that will permit them and will aid them to do what they have already made up their minds to do. Socrates, in his speculations, sought the right questions, including those he might never be able to answer and including those on which he would certainly need the guidance of God, either through an oracle at Delphi or through his *daimon's* veto or even through a dream. The difference between these two procedures may measure the distance between superstition and religion.

The Socrates we have just been listening to is the

Socrates who answered a charge of atheism before a court and was condemned to death; the Socrates in a prison cell who refused to let Crito save his life rather than "to fulfil the will of God, and to follow whither he leads"; and the Socrates in the same cell, during the last few hours of his life, who discussed the possible immortality of the soul and died in the hope that his own soul would not perish. But if we listen again to the Socrates of the *Symposium*, to the Socrates whom the drunken Alcibiades accused of inspiring in others his own madness, his passion for philosophy, his longing to understand, Socrates himself will try to tell us of another *daimon*, a great and mysterious *daimon*, who mediates between gods and men: Eros, the god of love.

The Greek word for banquet, *symposion*, meant a drinking together. Plato's *Symposium* describes a banquet at the home of the poet, Agathon, whose first tragedy had just won a prize. Several of Agathon's friends were invited, including Socrates. They had come to drink together; but, being Athenians, they remained to think together. One of them proposed that each banqueter in turn should make a speech in honor of Eros. Aristophanes, the comic poet, spoke humorously of the origins of the human race and of how, long ago, men had attempted to scale heaven and conquer the gods. Zeus, Aristophanes announced, punished these rebellious mortals by cutting their bodies in half lengthwise. But the god Love, a healer and helper of men, makes them long to be reunited. Love may act as sexual desire to reunite a man with a woman but Love may also draw human beings together in an attempt to recover a kind of community which Zeus, by way of punishing rebellion, had dispersed.

Agathon, the host, now took his turn. He chose to praise Love, not as mediator between gods and men but in and for himself. The greatest glory of Love, he said, is that he cannot suffer at the hands of force or violence except by his own consent. Nor does he use force or violence against others: only those serve him who serve by their own free will. And where there is voluntary agreement, there is justice. Agathon made it clear that the god Love was the true cause of such human virtues as courage, temperance, justice, and wisdom: "he is the fairest and best in himself, and the cause of what is fairest and best in all other things." He "gives peace on earth . . . sends courtesy and sends away discourtesy . . . gives kindness ever and never gives unkindness." He is "the friend of the good, the wonder of the wise, the amazement of the gods; desired by those who have no part in him, and precious to those who have the better part in him . . . in every word, work, wish, fear— saviour, pilot, comrade, helper . . . in whose footsteps let every man follow. . . . Such is the speech, Phaedrus, half-playful, yet having a certain measure of seriousness, which, according to my ability, I dedicate to the god." (Plato: *Symposium*, 197. Jowett.)

That ended Agathon's speech, and it was Socrates' turn. After affectionately questioning Agathon for a few minutes, he induced him to admit that Love essentially implies a lack, that Love is not a resplendent god but something else. Then he started telling his drinking companions how he once sought out a prophetess named Diotima, who knew all about Love. It was this wise woman who had told him that Love was not a god but "a great *daimon*" who interprets "between gods and men, conveying and taking across to the gods the prayers and sacrifices of men, and to men the commands and replies of the gods. . . . For God mingles not with man; but through Love all the intercourse and converse . . . is carried on." (Plato: *Symposium*, 202E-203A. Jowett.) And Diotima pictured Love as "neither mortal nor immortal," (Plato: *Symposium*, 202E. Jowett.) which was perhaps a paradoxical way of saying he was both God and man.

Love, Diotima told Socrates, is love of beauty, and more precisely of the birth or generation of beauty. Sexual desire is a desire to procreate, and procreation brings a kind of human immortality. Ultimately, Love is the love of immortality. This love of immortality not only generates children of the body, but children of the mind: poems, ideas, virtue, just laws. It is Love that leads us up a ladder of beauty, from sexual desire to a vision of Beauty itself. "But what if man had eyes to see the true beauty—the divine beauty, I mean, pure and clear and unalloyed, not clogged with the pollutions of mortality and all the colours and vanities of human life—thither looking, and holding converse with the true beauty simple and divine? Remember how in that communion only, beholding beauty with the eye of the mind, he will be enabled to bring forth, not images of beauty, but realities (for he has hold not of an image but of a reality), and bringing forth and nourishing true virtue to become the friend of God and be immortal, if mortal man may. Would that be an ignoble life?" (Plato: *Symposium*, 211E-212A. Jowett.)

So ended the mystical answer of Diotima the prophetess to Socrates' question, What is love? And when he had repeated it to his fellow banqueters, Socrates added that he believed her words were true. "And being persuaded of them, I try to persuade others, that in the attainment of this end human nature will not easily find a helper better than love. And therefore, also, I say that every man ought to honour him, as I myself honour him, and walk in his ways, and exhort others to do the same, and praise the power and spirit of love according to the measure of my ability now and ever." (Plato: *Symposium*, 212B. Jowett.) Socrates had scarcely uttered these last words of his encomium on Love when Alcibiades burst in and made his memorable speech on his own love for Socrates. The party turned to banter and to drinking. Socrates outdrank them all, and at cockcrow went to the Lyceum, "took a bath, and passed the day as usual. In the evening he retired to rest at his own home."

The speech in the *Symposium* is, of course, in one respect uncharacteristic of Socrates: he did not like speeches; he was a dialectical questioner not given to lecturing. On this occasion he was merely obeying the rules of the game, which required every man at the table to make a speech, on the same subject and on a subject Socrates had not chosen. In the *Apology*, it was the rules of the court procedure which required him to make a speech. On both occasions he made a declaration of faith. In court, he declared that, far from being an atheist, "I do believe that there are gods, and in a sense higher than that in which any of my accusers believe in them." In the *Symposium*, he reported what a wise woman, a prophetess, had told him Love really was, or else he playfully imagined a conversation that never took place. He was always fond of turning from argument to fable when he wanted to speak undogmatically of high matters. But he had no sooner reported, or imagined, Diotima's response to his question than he took care to state that he believed her.

In both speeches, he acknowledged his faith in and obedience to a *daimon*, or spirit. The *daimon* he acknowledged in court was a sort of guardian angel who merely vetoed false steps. But the *daimon* he acknowledged and hymned at Agathon's banquet was a sort of lord of all life who acted as intermediary between God and man, between all the gods and all men. This mediating *daimon* guided men towards some absolute Beauty, some absolute Truth, some absolute Good; and incidentally towards human happiness, the goal of all virtuous action. Indeed, this *daimon*, Eros, might lead a mortal man high enough to become "a friend of God" and to be himself "immortal, if mortal man may."

In his allegory of the cave, we recall, a man could be unchained and turned around by another. Those of us who undergo this conversion in real life are no longer doomed to fix all our attention on material things but can, perhaps at first dimly, see with the mind's eye the ideas which material things imperfectly embody. Stated allegorically, the unchained prisoner finally sees the carried objects of which he had hitherto seen only the shadows. Moreover, those of us who follow the ideas finally see them by a brighter intellectual light, just as in the allegory the unchained prisoner who ascends from the cave into sunlight sees material objects more clearly by sunlight than by flickering firelight. Those of us who persist in contemplating ideas may finally be able to contemplate the idea of the Good, the source of all ideas and all things, just as in the allegory the prisoner who learns to examine material objects in full sunlight with undazzled eyes finally learns to look at the source of all this light—that is, at the sun itself. The elaborate set of analogies embodied in this allegory leaves unanswered the questions: Who released the chained prisoner? And why did he want to "convert" or turn him around? Or, again, when Socrates insists on "compelling" the Guardians, or rulers, of his imagined Republic to turn from dialectic and contemplation and accept their tour of duty in practical political life, who or what can be trusted to compel them? He has already admitted that they will not wish to turn from study and contemplation to practical life in the moral and political spheres.

Will it not be the *daimon*, Eros, who compels them? And was it not Eros, Love, who directly or indirectly unchained the prisoner; turned him around so that he might see in a new way; and at last led him up to sunlight and even to look at the sun itself? But if Agathon

was right, Love would use neither force nor violence
to compel the Guardians to descend from speculation
and contemplation into the practical, the ethical, the
political arena, just as Love would have used neither
force nor violence to lead the unchained prisoner out
of the cave and into sunlight. Indeed Socrates himself,
who imagined both the Guardians and the unchained
prisoner, never used force on the notoriously violent
Alcibiades, who rushed unbidden and intoxicated into
Agathon's banquet hall and delivered his encomium on
Socrates in a tone of mock abuse: Socrates was a satyr,
a siren, a bully, and Alcibiades often wished that this
bully were dead, and he so mingled his praise and abuse
of the bully that Agathon and his guests laughed mer-
rily. Alcibiades knew Socrates loved him and by his
own confession Alcibiades had offered this satyr physical,
homosexual love. But the Eros that drew Socrates to
this gloriously beautiful and intellectually responsive
young man was an Eros of another sort. Socrates wanted
to lead Alcibiades out of the cave to which the young
man was repeatedly recalled by his love for fame and
power. Love for Alcibiades made Socrates want to encounter him intellectually and fully and to release from
somewhere inside this roisterer and demagogue the
philosophic mind which his own mind had discerned.
Whenever they met and talked, Socrates' gift for I-and-

thou communion subjected him, and the truth which they sought together in dialectic cruelly rebuked Alcibiades' political struggle for personal power. It was those encounters that made him love Socrates, and it was the pain of this rebuke that made him hate him.

It appears to be impossible to find in Aristotle the loving and intervening God of Socrates and Plato. In Aristotle, the universe God created yearns towards God, but God does not love or contemplate this universe: God contemplates and loves the one thing most worthy of contemplation and love—God. Nevertheless, Aristotle saw that the happiness of the good man is enhanced by friendship. Moreover, he saw that the polis, the human community organized under law, needs something more in its citizens than the moral virtues and even the intellectual virtues which Aristotle described in his *Nicomachean Ethics*. The good state needs friendship between its citizens. Centuries later, the French Revolution would proclaim that the state needs not only liberty and equality but fraternity. This humanitarian good will towards one's fellow-citizens may be a pale substitute for the great *daimon* Love, who was at least in part divine, and who served as an intermediary between gods and men. But we must recall that this *daimon*, Eros, guided men not only to the sexual desire which Alcibiades had vainly hoped his own physical

beauty would provoke in Socrates but also to the over-
whelming attraction of the intellectual beauty in dialectic and in I-and-thou encounter. We must recall that
Eros started with the physical attraction of one person's
beauty, but that this attraction was only the first rung
of a ladder that led upwards until the lover beheld a
vision of Beauty itself, a Beauty which had nothing
physical about it. Aristotle had his own ladder of love,
for he distinguished three sorts of friendship: the
friendship based on mutual utility; the friendship
based on the exchange of pleasures; and the friendship which he considered higher and more perma-
nent than either of these others, the friendship between
two good men, in which each desires for the other an
increase of virtue. In a truly good state, each citizen
would feel this third kind of friendship towards his
fellow-citizens. Feeling it, he would also be useful to
them and would give them pleasure too.

Centuries later St. Thomas Aquinas would construct
a Christian ethics on a double foundation, the moral
and intellectual virtues of the pagan Aristotle and the
theological virtues of St. Paul: faith, hope, and charity.
St. Thomas would hold that these three theological
virtues are not acquired by mere human effort but are
infused in men's souls by God and are acquired only
by grace. Of these three gifts from God, as St. Paul

pointed out, the greatest is charity. It is understandable
that Thomistic theology should find Aristotle's relative
omission of these three virtues and his relative omission
of grace a convenient philosophy on which to graft the
Pauline doctrine, in which words like grace, faith, hope,
and charity can be understood in the full context of
Christ's incarnation. But it is in Plato and not in Aristotle that one will find the closest analogues of grace
and of the three theological virtues of Thomistic doctrine. And it is not Aristotle's life, so far as we know
it, nor Plato's either, but the life of Socrates that has
moved men for many generations. Whether the Socrates
who aroused so much love among those who knew him
personally and who still arouses love among those who
read Plato did in historical fact do the things and say
the things which Plato reports him as doing and saying
is a question disputed by scholars and is largely a
matter of guesswork. But it ought to be clear that the
Socrates in Plato's Dialogues did not count on man's
human powers unaided by God's grace to bring him
to full happiness after his body's death and perhaps
did not count on them to be fully developed here on
earth without that same grace.

An indication that man's wisdom is insufficient to his
proper end is suggested by the very existence of that
tenth and last book of the *Republic*. Glaucon and Adei-

mantus, the two young brothers whose untutored philosophic ardor sustained Socrates' imaginative journey into Utopia, were anxious to be convinced not only that the truly just man is happier than the frankly unjust; not only that the just man is happier than he who, like Machiavelli's ideal prince, enjoys both the material advantages of injustice and the reputation of being just; but that the just man's reward of happiness is his during his lifetime and is not merely compensation in some other existence for his many sufferings here. When Socrates has convinced them even on this third point, why should not the *Republic* end? It does not. For at this point, once more, Socrates leaves dialectic and argument behind him and proceeds to tell a tale.

It seems that a Pamphylian named Er was slain in battle, but miraculously his body showed no decay. On the twelfth day it was laid on a funeral pyre, when suddenly Er returned to life and recounted what had happened to him—that is, to his separated soul—during the period since he had been killed. There follows a Dantesque description of Er's spiritual odyssey, of a kind of inferno, a kind of purgatory, and a kind of paradise; of judges, rewards, and punishments; of the Fates—the Three Sisters; and of a journey of a thousand years that souls must make before returning to life on earth. Then Socrates, who in philosophic matters eschewed exhortation in favor of the searching question, exhorted Glaucon and Adeimantus: "Wherefore my counsel is that we hold fast ever to the heavenly way and follow after virtue and justice always, considering that the soul is immortal and able to endure every sort of good and every sort of evil. Thus we shall live dear to one another and to the gods, both while remaining here and when, like conquerors in the games who go round to gather gifts, we receive our reward. And it shall be well with us both in this life and in the pilgrimage of a thousand years which we have been describing." (Plato: *Republic* X, 621C-D. Jowett.)

With these words Plato's *Republic,* together with Socrates' discourse therein, really does end. Socrates had embarked on his tale of Er lightly, as if the tale were a god ambiguously clothed in mist, a little in the same fashion in which he reported his conversation with Diotima about love, not asking us to believe either story. But, at the end of his tale about Er, he abruptly gave advice, as, after his tale of Diotima, he abruptly declared that he believed her. It will not help us much to say that Plato's writings are apparently full of Pythagorean doctrine, of the teachings issued in the Eleusinian mysteries, of the Orphic mysteries too. Surely, where a towering intellect first heard of an idea is never as important as the fact that this intellect made the idea its own.

The fact is that the Socrates of Plato's Dialogues did not emphasize, as Plato's pupil Aristotle did, that the moral virtues are habits, although he said they were. He was more interested in their dependence on what Aristotle called the intellectual virtues, and Aristotle agreed with him on this dependence. But Plato insisted, where Aristotle only faintly suggested, that the intellect is guided ultimately by God, since only God is truly wise. Like Aristotle he insisted that the man who would be truly effective in the world of action must learn to be effective in the world of thought; that the philosopher, the lover of wisdom, makes the best statesman and the best man. But he went far beyond Aristotle in insisting that the man who would be truly effective in this second world, the world of thought, must learn to live, so far as a man in this life can, in a third world, and that this third world is the world of grace in which God helps man. The world of thought exists independently of the world of moral action, but it penetrates the world of action, guides it, gives it meaning. The world of grace, the divine world, penetrates both the world of thought and the world of action, but the divine world exists and is good independently of both our human worlds. The Socrates whose life Plato reported, or half reported and half imagined, in his Dialogues, knew he lived both in the world of action and in the higher world of thought; he had faith that he lived partly in a third world, the divine world, and he had hope that he would one day live only in this other, third world; and it was this world that he most loved. On his unending quest to find the good of man in each of these three worlds, he calmly and confidently and lovingly staked all. No wonder that he acted as only those can act who possess the moral virtues. No wonder he thought as only those can think who possess the intellectual virtues. No wonder he prayed, trusted in God, hoped for another life, and loved his God. No wonder that his love of God seemed to him to help, not hinder, thinking, or that his love of wisdom seemed to him to help, not hinder, truly human action.

How deeply did Socrates believe in all three worlds? Enough, it seems, to die for them. But he was not given to insisting; he only strove to awaken.

Bibliographical Note

Most references are to the following books not fully identified in the notes:

The Loeb Classical Library (texts and translations of Greek and Latin authors, now published in this country by Harvard University Press) .

Plato: *The Dialogues of Plato*. Translated by Benjamin Jowett, 2 vols. New York: Random House, 1937.